KU-197-199

another
3 padlocks

5 more black
spiders

1 other
plane

5 more
yellow butterflies

a sleeping
joey like this

another
3 snakes

Where's my missing slipper?

another
3 combs

3 more spotted
toadstools

a squirrel
just like this

Which bushbaby has blue eyes?

Find someone carrying a candle.

Can you find...

3 more pineapples

5 other bugs like this

another 3 pink
spiders

2 more
caterpillars

another plate
of pizza

Can you find... another upside-down mouse   3 more snails, all different

10

another 2
fish like this

5 more
dragonflies

another little
yellow bird

Who is wearing a sweater?

Spot someone having a drink.

Can you find...

7 red ants like this

another 3 bats

14

Find two cubs underneath their mother.

Can you find...

another 4 squirrels

2 more lanterns

16

Can you find...

3 more
buckets

another 2
of these

3 more plants
like this

5 more
white flowers

another centipede
like this

a pink ribbon
just like this

5 more
blue stars

another 2 cups
and saucers

21

Spot a squirrel wearing a bow tie.

Can you find another owl like me?

Can you find...

2 other nests

4 more star decorations

Who's having a bedtime story?

another 3
pink striped hats

1 more
blue scarf

another bird
like this

23

Can you see my spotted blanket?

Can you find...

8 more flying white birds

2 other snakes

24

another
laughing hyena

5 more birds
just like this

2 lizards
like this

Answers

Cover

2–3

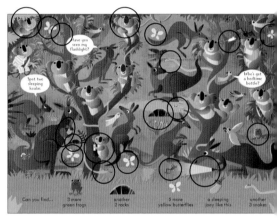

4–5

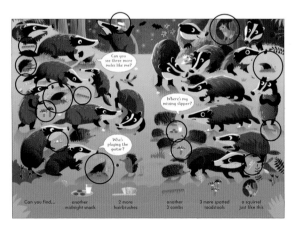

6–7

8–9

10–11

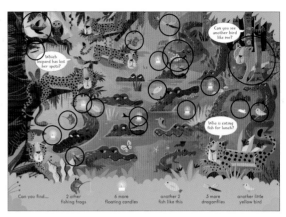

12–13

14–15

16–17

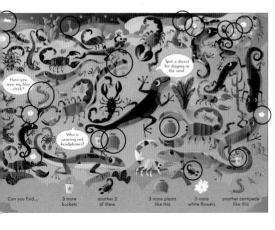

18–19

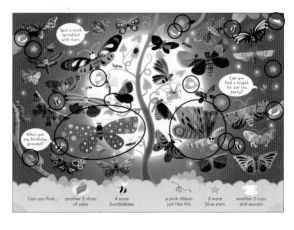

20–21

22-23

24-25

26-27

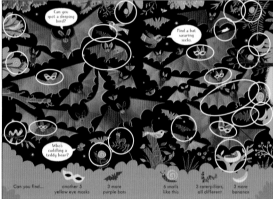

28-29

First published in 2021 by Usborne Publishing Ltd, Usborne House, 83-85 Saffron Hill, London, EC1N 8RT, England. usborne.com ©2021 Usborne Publishing Ltd. The name Usborne and the Balloon logos are trade marks of Usborne Publishing Ltd. All rights reserved. No part of this publication may be reproduced, stored in a retrieval system, or transmitted in any form or by any means without the prior permission of the publisher. UE. Printed in China.